MY FIRST LOOK AT COUNTRIES

AUSTRALIA HAS LOTS OF OPEN LAND

Australia

ADELE RICHARDSON

CREATIVE EDUCATION

Published by Creative Education

123 South Broad Street, Mankato, Minnesota 56001

Creative Education is an imprint of The Creative Company

Designed by Rita Marshall

Photographs by Getty Images (Paul Chesley, Jeff Hunter, Jiri Lochman, Ted Mead, David

Noton, Mitch Reardon, Penny Tweedie, Robert Van Der Hilst, Simon Wilkinson, Karen

Wilson / Tostee.com, Art Wolfe)

Printed in the United States of America

Library of Congress Cataloging-in-Publication Data

Richardson, Adele, 1966- Australia / by Adele Richardson.

p. cm. — (My first look at countries)

Includes bibliographical references.

ISBN-13 : 978-1-58341-443-9

I. Australia—Juvenile literature. I. Title.

DU96.R5325 2006   994—dc22   2005051763

First edition 9 8 7 6 5 4 3 2 1

AUSTRALIA

THE LAND DOWN UNDER

People call Australia "the land down under." That is because of where it is found. Australia is down under the **equator** (*ee-KWAY-ter*). It is in the bottom part of the world.

In Australia, the **seasons** happen at different times of the year than in the top part of the world. Winter is in June, July, and August. Summer is in December and January. That means Christmas comes in the summer!

AUSTRALIA IS NEAR THE BOTTOM OF MAPS

Australia is not just the name of a country. It is the name of a **continent**, too. Australia is the smallest continent. No other countries touch Australia. On a map, it looks like a big island!

Outback and Cities

The middle part of Australia is **desert**. It is hot and dry. People in Australia call it the "outback." Few people live in the outback.

Australia does not get
much rain. It is the driest
continent on Earth.

A BIG, COLORFUL ROCK IN THE OUTBACK

Most people in Australia live on the east side. East is the right side of Australia on a map. Australia's **capital** is on the east side. It is called Canberra (*CAN-bur-ruh*). Canberra is one of the biggest cities in Australia.

Most of Australia's big cities are near the ocean. After work or school, people in Australia like to play! Many swim or surf in the ocean. Others hike or ride bikes.

In Australia, a nosy

person might be called

a "sticky beak!"

AWESOME ANIMALS

Many kinds of animals live in Australia. Dogs and snakes live there. So do crocodiles. Lots of birds live in Australia, too. One big bird is the emu. It can grow as tall as a man! Emus have wings, but they cannot fly.

Some animals in Australia have a pouch on their belly. Kangaroos have a pouch on their belly. So do koalas. Their babies ride in the pouch.

KOALAS LIVE HIGH IN AUSTRALIA'S TREES

Lots of animals swim in the ocean near Australia. Colorful fish swim in the water. There are sharks, too. Sea turtles swim near Australia. So do big whales.

A SEA TURTLE SWIMMING NEAR AUSTRALIA

FRIENDLY PEOPLE

"G-day mate!" That is how people in Australia say hello. G-day is short for "good day." Mate means "friend."

The first people to live in Australia were the Aborigines (*ab-uh-RIJ-in-eez*). Aborigines have dark hair and skin. They have lived in Australia for a very long time. Today, some Aborigines live in the outback. Others live in cities.

Aborigines invented the
boomerang. They used
it as a hunting tool.

THE OUTBACK CAN BE A LONELY PLACE

Lots of people go to Australia every year. They like to see all of the animals. Some people go to the outback. They can take a train ride across the desert. Other people go to Australia's cities. No matter where they go, they meet friendly people!

Australia is the only

country with wild camels.

They live in the desert.

WILD CAMELS RUN ACROSS DESERT SANDS

HANDS-ON: CAVE ART

Aborigines used to paint on the walls of caves. Here is a way to make your own cave art!

WHAT YOU NEED

Crayons
A piece of sandpaper, any size
Tape

WHAT YOU DO

1. Lay the sandpaper on the floor or a table. Make sure the rough side is up.
2. Draw a picture on the sandpaper. Cave art can be people, animals, circles, or curvy lines. Draw whatever you would like. You may have to press hard on the sandpaper.
3. Tape your art to the wall. Invite others to see your cave art!

SOME CAVE ART IN AUSTRALIA SHOWS ANIMALS

INDEX

WORDS TO KNOW

capital—the main city in a country

continent—one of Earth's seven big pieces of land

desert—a dry, sandy area where few plants and trees grow

equator—the make-believe line that separates the top and bottom parts of Earth

seasons—the four parts of the year: spring, summer, fall, and winter

READ MORE

Bagley, Katie. *Australia*. Mankato, Minn.: Bridgestone Books, 2003.

Donaldson, Madeline. *Australia*. Minneapolis: Lerner Publications, 2005.

Sayre, April Pulley. *G'Day Australia!* Brookfield, Conn.: Millbrook Press, 2003.

EXPLORE THE WEB

Australia For Kids http://www2.lhric.org/pocantico/australia/australia.htm

Kip and Co. http://www.kipandco.com.au

Zoom School: Australia http://www.enchantedlearning.com/school/Australia